Little People, BIG DREAMS
WILMA RUDOLPH

Written by
Mª Isabel Sánchez Vegara

Illustrated by
Amelia Flower

Frances Lincoln
Children's Books

One summer day, a little baby arrived to a big and loving family. Her name was Wilma and she was the tiniest baby in Tennessee, or so her 19 siblings thought...

Wilma caught almost every disease that came through town. But things got even worse when she was just four: one day, her left leg began to turn in and become twisted.

She had contracted an illness called polio, and doctors said she would never walk again without a leg brace.

But her mother told Wilma that she would.
And Wilma decided to believe her.

Maybe Wilma needed her brace to move around for now, but she promised herself that, one day, she would run even faster than a gazelle.

Twice a week, Wilma and her mom would go to the hospital.
They had to sit tight at the back of the bus for two long hours,
while white passengers sat comfortably at the front.
But they never missed an appointment.

Back home, her brothers and sisters would take turns rubbing her leg, just like the nurses did at the hospital. For five years, they gave Wilma four massages nearly every day. That's around 7,300 massages!

Finally, her family's care and attention showed results: by the time she was nine, Wilma no longer needed her leg brace. And once she took it off, there was no turning back.

She had always wanted to play basketball, so the first thing she did was ask for a chance to join the girls' high school team.

Wilma scored 803 points in less than a year, setting a record and leading her team to the state championship.

One day, a coach named Ed spotted Wilma playing and invited her to join a summer college program for young athletes. Soon, she was running so fast that, if you blinked, you may have missed her.

She was the youngest member of the US team
at the Olympic Games in Australia, where she won
her first bronze medal running the 400-meter relay.
But she knew that, next time, she would do even better.

Four years later, Wilma went to the Olympics in Rome:
she became the first woman to win three gold medals.
Her success made many girls realize that sprinting
was not something only boys could do.

When she returned home, the governor planned to hold a welcome parade for her. Wilma attended under one single condition: people of all colors should join the celebration as one.

And many athletes found inspiration in the
story of little Wilma. The girl who fought against
all odds to become the fastest woman in the world.
The one who knew greatness lives within each of us.

WILMA RUDOLPH

(Born 1940 • Died 1994)

c. 1960   1960

Wilma Rudolph was born a preemie, in Tennessee, as the 20th of 22 children. She weighed just four and a half pounds when she was born. As a child, she caught pneumonia, scarlet fever, and then polio. She survived polio, but it made her left leg paralyzed, and she needed a leg brace to walk. Wilma's family didn't have much money, so she had to travel on a segregated bus to a hospital 50 miles away to receive weekly treatment. At home, her older siblings massaged her leg to get the blood flowing. Doctors said she wouldn't walk again, but her mother told her she would. Her mother was right. Through the dedication of her family, and Wilma's own determination, the treatment worked. After five years, she took her leg brace off and walked by herself. By the time she was 12, she had challenged every boy in her neighborhood to a race. Wilma then joined

1963   1969

her school basketball team and was scouted by an athletics coach. In four
seasons, she never lost a single race. By 1960, she was ready to go to the
Olympics in Rome. She won all three of her gold medals in the 100- and
200-meter sprints, and also the 400-meter relay. Her achievements were
groundbreaking: she was the first American woman to win three gold
medals in one Olympics, and was nicknamed "Gazelle." She challenged
what people thought was possible for women to achieve in athletics. When
she returned home, she used her success to insist that any celebratory
parades had to be integrated (rather than segregated). Wilma retired from
athletics on a high. She graduated from college and spent the rest of her life
teaching the next generation that they could do anything.

Want to find out more about **Wilma Rudolph?**
Read one of these great books:

Wilma Unlimited by Kathleen Krull and David Diaz

Wilma Rudolph: Olympic Runner by Jo Harper and Meryl Henderson

When Wilma Rudolph Played Basketball by Mark Weakland and Daniel Duncan

BOARD BOOKS

COCO CHANEL

ISBN: 978-1-78603-245-4

MAYA ANGELOU
ISBN: 978-1-78603-249-2

FRIDA KAHLO
ISBN: 978-1-78603-247-8

AMELIA EARHART
ISBN: 978-1-78603-252-2

MARIE CURIE

ISBN: 978-1-78603-253-9

ADA LOVELACE
ISBN:978-1-78603-259-1

ROSA PARKS
ISBN: 978-1-78603-263-8

EMMELINE PANKHURST

ISBN: 978-1-78603-261-4

AUDREY HEPBURN
ISBN: 978-1-78603-255-3

ELLA FITZGERALD
ISBN:978-1-78603-257-7

BOX SETS

WOMEN IN ART

ISBN: 978-1-78603-428-1

WOMEN IN SCIENCE
ISBN: 978-1-78603-429-8

BOOKS & PAPER DOLLS

EMMELINE PANKHURST
ISBN: 978-1-78603-400-7

MARIE CURIE
ISBN: 978-1-78603-401-4

Collect the
Little People, **BIG DREAMS** series:

FRIDA KAHLO

ISBN: 978-1-84780-783-0

COCO CHANEL

ISBN: 978-1-84780-784-7

MAYA ANGELOU

ISBN: 978-1-84780-889-9

AMELIA EARHART

ISBN: 978-1-84780-888-2

AGATHA CHRISTIE

ISBN: 978-1-84780-960-5

MARIE CURIE

ISBN: 978-1-84780-962-9

ROSA PARKS

ISBN: 978-1-78603-018-4

AUDREY HEPBURN

ISBN: 978-1-78603-053-5

EMMELINE PANKHURST

ISBN: 978-1-78603-020-7

ELLA FITZGERALD
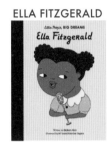
ISBN: 978-1-78603-087-0

ADA LOVELACE

ISBN: 978-1-78603-076-4

JANE AUSTEN

ISBN: 978-1-78603-120-4

GEORGIA O'KEEFFE

ISBN: 978-1-78603-122-8

HARRIET TUBMAN
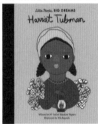
ISBN: 978-1-78603-227-0

ANNE FRANK

ISBN: 978-1-78603-229-4

MOTHER TERESA

ISBN: 978-1-78603-230-0

JOSEPHINE BAKER

ISBN: 978-1-78603-228-7

L. M. MONTGOMERY

ISBN: 978-1-78603-233-1

JANE GOODALL

ISBN: 978-1-78603-231-7

SIMONE DE BEAUVOIR

ISBN: 978-1-78603-232-4

MUHAMMAD ALI

ISBN: 978-1-78603-331-4

STEPHEN HAWKING

ISBN: 978-1-78603-333-8

MARIA MONTESSORI

ISBN: 978-1-78603-755-8

VIVIENNE WESTWOOD

ISBN: 978-1-78603-757-2

MAHATMA GANDHI

ISBN: 978-1-78603-787-9

DAVID BOWIE

ISBN: 978-1-78603-332-1

WILMA RUDOLPH

ISBN: 978-1-78603-751-0

DOLLY PARTON

ISBN: 978-1-78603-760-2

Brimming with creative inspiration, how-to projects, and useful information to enrich your everyday life, Quarto Knows is a favorite destination for those pursuing their interests and passions. Visit our site and dig deeper with our books into your area of interest: Quarto Creates, Quarto Cooks, Quarto Homes, Quarto Lives, Quarto Drives, Quarto Explores, Quarto Gifts, or Quarto Kids.

Text © 2019 Mª Isabel Sánchez Vegara. Illustrations © 2019 Amelia Flower.

First Published in the UK in 2019 by Frances Lincoln Children's Books, an imprint of The Quarto Group.

400 First Avenue North, Suite 400, Minneapolis, MN 55401, USA.

T (612) 344-8100 F (612) 344-8692 **www.QuartoKnows.com**

First Published in Spain in 2019 under the title Pequeña & Grande Wilma Rudolph.

by Alba Editorial, s.l.u., Baixada de Sant Miquel, 1, 08002 Barcelona

www.albaeditorial.es

All rights reserved.

Published by arrangement with Alba Editorial, s.l.u. Translation rights arranged by IMC Agència Literària, SL

A catalog record for this book is available from the British Library.

ISBN 978-1-78603-751-0

The illustrations were created digitally on an iPad Pro.

Set in Futura BT.

Published by Rachel Williams • Designed by Karissa Santos

Edited by Katy Flint • Production by Jenny Cundill

Manufactured in Guangdong, China CC032019

9 7 5 3 1 2 4 6 8

Photographic acknowledgments (pages 28–29, from left to right) 1. Sprinter Wilma Rudolph alone during practice, c. 1960 © David Lees / Contributor.com via Getty Images 2. Wilma Rudolph, 1960. © Mark Kauffman / Contributor via Getty Images 3. Olympic Gold Medal Winner Wilma Rudolph Graduating from College, 1963 © Bettmann / Contributor via Getty Images 4. Olympian Wilma Rudolph, 1969 © Bettmann via Getty Images